THIS BOOK BELONGS TO:

Josh love from shep Marg

© LOONART

Other books by Patricia St John

The Tanglewoods' Secret
Treasures of the Snow
Star of Light
The Other Kitten
Friska my Friend
The Secret of the Fourth Candle
Rainbow Garden
The Mystery of Pheasant Cottage
The Victor
I Needed a Neighbour
Nothing Else Matters
A King is Born – The Christmas Story
A King is Risen – The Easter Story

STORIES THAT JESUS TOLD

THE PARABLES RETOLD FOR CHILDREN
BY PATRICIA ST. JOHN

Illustrated by Tony Morris

Jesus loved to teach people by telling them parables.
A parable is a story with a hidden meaning.

MOREHOUSE PUBLISHING

Copyright © 1993 Angus Hudson Ltd/Three's Company
Text copyright © 1993 Patricia St. John
First published in 1994.

First published in Great Britain by Candle Books 1994

First published in the United States of America by
Morehouse Publishing

Editorial Office:
871 Ethan Allen Hwy.
Ridgefield, CT 06877

Corporate Office:
P.O. Box 1321
Harrisburg, PA 17105

ISBN: 0–8192–1644–5

Library of Congress Cataloging-in-Publication Data:
St. John, Patricia Mary, 1919–
    Stories that Jesus told : the parables retold for children / by
Patricia St. John : [illustrated by Tony Morris].
        p.   cm.
    Originally published: London : Candle Books, 1994.
    Summary: Presents eighteen parables of Jesus retold for
children including the missing sheep, the unforgiving servant,
and the good neighbor.
    ISBN 0–8192–1644–5 (pbk.)
    1. Jesus Christ—Parables—Juvenile literature. 2. Bible
stories, English—N.T. Gospels. [1. Jesus
Christ—Parables. 2. Parables. 3. Bible stories—N.T.]
I. Morris, Tony, ill. II. Title.
BT376.S72   1995
226.8′08505—dc20   95–7421
                                                              CIP
                                                              AC

Printed in Singapore

Contents

The busy farmer

How should we listen?

JESUS loved to teach people by telling them parables. A parable is a story with a hidden meaning.

One day Jesus sat on the hillside by the Lake of Galilee. The birds were singing and the farmers in the fields around were planting their grain. A crowd of people sat on the grass round him listening as he taught them how God wanted them to live – lovingly, honestly, learning about him.

Some were half asleep.

Some thought, "It sounds very difficult."

Others thought, "I would never have time to do that."

But some said to themselves, "This is how I want to live."

So Jesus told them a story. He pointed to the farmer. "Watch the farmer sowing his seed," he said. "Look! Some of it is falling on the hard, stony path. It can't grow there. Look again! The birds are swooping down to eat it.

"But watch the farmer now. Some of the seed is falling on that dry patch of ground where no one has watered. It may start to grow, but it will soon wither when the sun gets really hot.

"The farmer is moving on; he's flung a handful of seed into that patch of weeds. It may take root, but it won't have room to grow. The weeds will choke it.

"Ah, but now he has reached the good part of the field! There are no stones or weeds here, and someone has watered it. The soil is soft and damp. The farmer will get a wonderful harvest from this part of the field."

Evening came and the people went home. But the disciples gathered round Jesus. "Tell us what the story meant," they asked. "We didn't understand."

5

"Then I'll explain," said Jesus. "The farmer is like me. The seed he sowed is like the words I speak. The ground is like the hearts of the people who listen.

"Some people's hearts are like stony ground; they hardly listen at all. If someone asks them what they have heard, they answer, 'I've forgotten.'

"Some other people are like the patch of weeds. They like what they hear. They start to follow Jesus and learn more about God. But it takes time to read the Bible and pray. These people have too much to do, too many people to talk to, too many games to play. 'I'm giving up,' they say after a time. 'I'm too busy!'

"Others are rather like the seeds that withered when the sun got too hot. They listen and they say, 'That's good; we want to be like that.' And they go home and start trying. But it is not easy to be kind and honest and good, and after a time they get tired of it. 'I'm not bothering any longer,' they say. 'It's too difficult.'

"But I'm so glad that some people really listen," said Jesus. "Their hearts are like good ground. They listen and remember. They keep on being loving and honest, even when it is very difficult. Even though they are busy people, they make time to read the Bible and pray. Their lives will grow beautiful and strong and useful. God will be pleased with them."

The discontented son

Does God love people who do wrong?

JESUS came to earth to show us what God is like. But there was something about him that well-behaved people could not understand. He was always talking to rough, dishonest people. One day they asked him why.

"Where will you find a doctor?" replied Jesus. "Among well people or ill people? I came specially to tell the people who do wrong that God loves them. He will forgive them and help them to be good."

Then Jesus told two stories to show how God loves to forgive those who are sorry for doing wrong.

"There was once a farmer who had two sons. The younger son was always grumbling. One day he said to his father, 'I know that when you die you will leave me some money. Could I have it now?'

"The father felt very sad, but he gave the boy the money. The boy was delighted. 'Bye dad, bye brother!' he shouted. 'I'm off to enjoy myself in town!'

"As he had plenty of money, the younger son soon made friends. It was easy to make friends when he paid for all the treats. *What a nice guy I must be,* he thought. *Everybody likes me.*

"But money does not last forever, and the day came when there was none left. He told his friends. But next day none of them wanted to know him. Then the boy understood; they didn't like him at all. They only liked his money.

"*I'll have to beg,* thought the boy. But nobody gave him anything and his so-called friends just laughed at him. No one cared.

"'I'll have to find work,' said the boy. And he wandered out into the country.

"Suddenly he heard a loud, snorty, gobbly noise. He turned round and saw a herd of pigs gobbling up pigswill. The boy was so hungry that he wished he could get down on all fours and share their meal.

"Along came the farmer. 'Any work?' asked the boy.

"'You can mind the pigs,' said the farmer. 'I'll pay you tonight.'

"It was a long, hungry day. The boy sat watching the pigs, half awake and half dreaming. He seemed to be seeing the green fields of his own farm and the kind face of his father.

"*What a fool I've been!* he thought. *Even the servants at home have plenty to eat – while I starve... I'm going home. I'll say, 'Father, I've sinned against God and you, and I don't deserve to be your son. Just let me be a servant.'*

"So he started out on the long journey home.

"But his father had never forgotten him. Every morning he climbed to the flat roof of the house and gazed down the road. *Perhaps today my son will come home,* he thought.

"Then one morning the father noticed someone far away. He shaded his eyes and stared. Yes, even ragged and barefoot, he knew his son. 'It's him!' he cried and tore out of the house.

"'Whatever's happened?' asked the servants. And they ran too.

"But the father got there first, and flung his arms round his son.

"'Father!' gasped the boy. 'I have sinned against God and you, and I don't deserve to be your son…' But he never finished his speech because his father was holding him tight and shouting joyfully to the servants.

"'Go and bring some beautiful clothes, and shoes, and a ring and make a big feast! For it's just as though my son had died and has now come back to life again! He was lost and is found.' Joyfully, joyfully he led his son home.

"In the same way," said Jesus, "there is joy in the presence of the angels of God when someone is sorry and comes home to God's love."

The missing sheep

Does God really care about me?

ONE bright morning a shepherd led his flock out to pasture. He walked ahead, and the sheep followed close behind. There were snakes and wild animals and birds of prey in that country, and it was important to keep close to the shepherd.

Only one young sheep lagged behind. Why always go to the same pasture? The grass looked so green and the wild flowers so pretty over to the left. No one would notice if he went exploring.

He slipped behind a rock and soon reached the green field he had seen. The grass was delicious and he could see a little stream further on. He skipped along, but it was getting very hot ... just a little further ... Then he saw some shady rocks. He curled up under the shade of one of them and went to sleep.

The sheep slept for a long time. When he woke the sun was going down. He felt very frightened.

I must get back to the flock, he thought. But he could not remember which way he had come. *I'm lost!* thought the sheep. *What shall I do?*

The sun disappeared and it was getting dark. Somewhere among the rocks a wolf howled. The sheep began to run wildly, but he was running the wrong way. It was now so dark that he could not see a path at all. There seemed to be no more grass, only stones and thorn bushes.

Tired and very cold, he lay down under a rock. *There's no hope for me at all,* he thought, *unless my shepherd comes to look for me. But he has so many sheep; why should he care about a silly, disobedient sheep like me?*

Meanwhile the shepherd had led the rest of the flock to another green field, with a stream flowing through it. The sheep grazed peacefully till the sky grew red with the setting sun. Then they followed the shepherd home.

One by one they entered the sheepfold, and one by one the shepherd counted them in. "Ninety-seven, ninety-eight, ninety-nine … This can't be the last! I know I set out with one hundred sheep."

He counted again; but there was no mistake. One was missing.

It was nearly dark, but he fetched his stick and his lantern.

"Where are you going?" asked the neighbors.

"I'm going to find my lost sheep," answered the shepherd.

"But it's dangerous out there. Why bother? You have many others."

"I love my sheep," answered the shepherd. "And this one needs me."

So off he went. It was cold and dark, and he too heard the wolf howling. Sometimes he stumbled on sharp rocks; sometimes thorns tore his hands. "But I'm not going home till I find my lost sheep," said the shepherd.

Suddenly he stood still; he could hear a faint bleat.

"That's him!" cried the shepherd, and, guided by the bleating, he found the lost animal. Joyfully he picked up the frightened sheep and laid it across his shoulders. It was almost morning when they got home and the neighbors were waking up.

"Let's have a party," said the tired shepherd. "I have found my lost sheep."

"What a fuss over one," thought the neighbors. But to the shepherd every one was loved and important.

However small you may be, God loves you.

The selfish farmers

Why did Jesus die?

LONG before Jesus came to earth, God sent messengers called prophets to teach people God's way of love, goodness and truth. But most people would not listen. They wanted to go on living as they pleased, and they often killed the prophets. Many people would not listen to Jesus either. So he told this story.

"A farmer planted a beautiful vineyard. But he had to go away, so he rented it out to other farmers. He arranged for them to share the grapes with him when they were ripe.

"Summer came, and the fruit grew ripe and sweet. It was nearly time to pick the grapes, when one day some men arrived at the vineyard. They had come a long way.

"'Good morning,' they said very politely. 'Our master sent us to collect his share of the grapes.'

"'You're joking!' said the farmers. 'Tell your master the vineyard belongs to us now. We're keeping the lot!'

"The servants tried to reason with them, but it was no good. The farmers took sticks and stones and beat them until they fled back home.

"The owner of the vineyard was sad and angry. But he was a patient man. 'I'll send a bigger group of my servants,' he said. 'I'll give the farmers one more chance.'

"But the farmers did not want another chance. They wanted the grapes. They beat up the second group of servants, and even killed one of them. The rest went home bruised and empty-handed.

"The owner of the vineyard was very, very sad, but he wanted to give the farmers one more chance.

"'I'll send my son,' he said. 'They will respect him, and he will bring me my grapes.'

"The son was willing to go, even though he knew what the farmers were like. 'I'll go, father,' he said. 'It is good to give them one more chance.'

"So the son went alone to tell the farmers that they were forgiven, and to ask them to make peace.

"But it didn't work out like that. When they saw him, the farmers had other ideas.

"'So this is the one to whom the vineyard will belong!' said one.

"'Let's kill him,' whispered another. 'The master won't try again, and the vineyard will belong to us for ever.'

"And they seized the son and killed him. But they never enjoyed the grapes, and there were no more chances. The owner came with an army and destroyed them all."

And what the farmers did is exactly what people did to Jesus, God's son, to whom the world belonged. He came to teach us God's way, even though other messengers had been killed. But when he came the people mostly wanted to go on in their own way of selfishness, lies and unhappiness; and so they put him to death.

But of course they really had no power over him at all. He came to die, to take the punishment for all the wrong things we have done. He died so that we might be forgiven. His enemies did not know that he would rise again, and that one day the whole world would know about God's way. God has given us another chance.

17

The unforgiving servant

How often should we forgive?

JESUS' disciples had been quarrelling about which of them was the most important, even though Jesus had told them that gentle, unselfish people were the greatest in God's sight.

"If someone goes on being mean to me over and over again," said Peter, "how often have I got to forgive him?"

"I'll answer by telling you a story," said Jesus.

"A servant was supposed to pay money to the king every week, like everyone else. After all, he lived on the king's land and farmed the king's fields.

"But he was a lazy fellow and couldn't be bothered to work. Time after time when the king's messenger came for the money, the servant would say, 'Sorry, nothing this week. I'll make it up next week.' After all, the king was known to be a kind man. So the man owed more and more money.

"Then one day a message came. The servant was to go to the palace at once and pay up. He was terribly frightened, and soon stood trembling before the king.

"'Where are my 10,000 silver coins?' asked the king sternly.

"'Please, your majesty,' whispered the servant, 'I haven't got anything!'

"'Then you will have to be my slave,' said the king. 'And your wife and children will become slaves. There is no other way of paying your debt.'

"The servant fell on his knees. He just could not bear it.

"'Please, please wait,' he sobbed. 'I'll save up. Just give me more time.'

"The king looked sadly at the servant. He knew he would never be able to pay up, and he felt very sorry for him. 'I'll give you one more chance,' the king said gently. 'This time I'll let you off repaying the money.'

"The servant was delighted. He almost danced out of the palace. He was free! The kind king had forgiven him all those years of debt. But just outside the palace he saw another servant, and suddenly he remembered!

"I once lent that man a hundred silver coins, he thought – *and he never paid me back. I'll get it off him right now.* He rushed across the road and seized the servant by the collar. 'What about that money?' he growled.

"The man was terrified. 'Please, please wait!' he cried. 'I'll save up. Just give me more time.'

"'There's no more time,' yelled the servant. 'You can go to prison until you pay!'

"But the servant forgot that he was very close to the palace, and someone was watching. That person went straight to the king and told him what had happened.

"'Call that servant back,' said the king.

"The servant was scared. *Me?* he thought. *What could he want with me again?* He went back and stood in front of the king. But the king no longer looked kind and forgiving. He looked very angry.

"'You cruel man,' said the king. 'Didn't I forgive you that great big debt? And you wouldn't even forgive a tiny debt. You don't deserve to be forgiven at all. You, too, will stay in prison until you can pay.'"

How many times has God forgiven you? Over and over and over again! So that's how often we ought to forgive each other.

The good neighbor

Who needs my help?

JESUS was once teaching his disciples about loving God and loving their neighbors. A man in the crowd stood up and asked, "Who is my neighbor?"

So Jesus told a story.

"A man started out on a journey from Jerusalem up in the hills to Jericho down in the valley. It was a lonely road that wound downhill between rocks. Thieves lurked among the rocks, so it was a dangerous road.

"This man travelled alone and carried money, so you can guess what happened. Out rushed thieves, seized his purse, hit him with sticks, stole his clothes and made off. The traveller lay in the road bleeding, too hurt and bruised to get up.

"'Help, help!' he cried. But it was a wild and lonely road and nobody heard him.

"At last he heard footsteps on the road. 'Help!' he screamed. 'Please help me!'

"The man who came down the road was well dressed. He looked at the poor man lying there, and noticed all the blood. *If I stop to help this poor fellow,* he thought, *I might spoil my nice coat.* So he pretended not to see and hurried past.

"*I shall die,* thought the traveller.

"But listen! More footsteps on the road. The traveller was feeling tired and faint by now, but he managed to call, 'Help! help!'

"The man coming along was in a hurry. He too glanced at the traveller and heard his cry. 'If I stop and help him, I'll be late,' said the man. 'I'll pretend not to hear.' And he hurried past as well.

"*Now I really shall die,* thought the poor traveller, *and nobody cares.* He was in great pain and very thirsty, and the day was getting hotter and hotter. Then he heard another sound; not footsteps this time, but the clip-clop of a little donkey.

"The traveller was too weak to shout any more. He just whispered, 'Help me, oh please help me!'

"The man riding on the donkey heard his whisper. He was a stranger in that part of the country. He looked at the traveller lying in the road, then hurried over and knelt beside him.

"'Poor fellow,' he said. 'I will try and help you.'

"He took his pack from the donkey's back. In the pack were medicine and bandages and something to drink. Very carefully he bound up the traveller's wounds, and very gently he helped him onto the donkey.

"The stranger walked along holding the traveller on the donkey. There was a little hotel down the road. They went very slowly, but they reached the hotel at last. The hotel-keeper came running out, and together they helped the poor traveller to bed. Of course he had no money. It had all been stolen.

"'Never mind,' said the stranger to the hotel-keeper. 'Here's some money. Tomorrow I will have to go on, but look after this poor man till he's better. On my way back, I'll pay for everything.'

"Which of those three helped the poor traveller?" asked Jesus.

"The third," said the man who had asked the question.

"Right!" said Jesus. "Now go and be like that third man. Your neighbor is anyone who needs your love and help."

The worried disciples

Why worry?

JESUS quite often climbed up into the hills to teach his disciples quietly, away from the crowds. On one special day in spring the flowers were blooming and the birds were singing. Jesus was telling his disciples that real happiness comes, not from having things, but from doing what is right.

Many people think the way to be happy is to have lots of money, lots of clothes and lots of food. So of course they are always worried in case they lose their money. Jesus was talking about people like that.

He pointed to a bird singing nearby. "Look at that bird," he said. "He can't grow corn or work in the fields, like you can. But he doesn't worry. He knows that God, his Heavenly Father, will feed him.

"So why do you, who can work and grow food, worry about what you are going to eat? If God feeds that helpless little bird, can't you trust him to feed you?"

Then Jesus pointed to a beautiful wild lily. "Look at that flower," he said. "No king ever wore clothes as beautiful as the white petals of that lily. Yet the lily can't stitch and sew like you can. So why do you worry about your clothes? If God dresses that lily so beautifully, won't he also care for you?"

If we are not to worry about money, food or clothes, what are we to worry about? Well, if you know that you belong to your Heavenly Father, and are trusting him and living to please him, you need not worry at all. He is the perfect Father, and he will always love and care for his own children.

The two builders

What happens when things are difficult?

JESUS looked again at the people who crowded round him. Some were hardly listening at all; but others were listening to every word, so he spoke to them. He told them a story.

"One summer day a man wanted to build a house. So he cut into the rock and laid a strong foundation. Then he built his house on top. 'Now I shall be safe when the storms come,' he said. 'I've nothing to worry about.'

"His friend also wanted to build a house, but he was rather lazy. 'It's much easier to build on the sand,' he said. 'And my house looks just as good as yours.'

"'Well, yes,' answered the first man. 'But it's summer now. What about winter, when the wind blows and the waves come roaring up the beach? What then?'

"'I'm not bothered about that,' said his friend. 'It's still summer. Let's enjoy ourselves.'

28

"Autumn came, and the nights grew longer. The first man was calm, trusting in his strong foundation. The second man started to worry. His house seemed to be getting a bit wobbly.

"Then one black night a storm broke. The rain came down in torrents, the wind howled over the sea and the tide came racing up the sand.

"Dawn broke grey and cold. High on the rock the little house stood battered but firm; but down on the beach were just a few scattered boards and bricks. Most of that building had been carried away by the waves of the sea."

"Listen to me and do what I say," said Jesus. "Then, when hard times and difficulties come, you will trust in me. I will keep you safe and unafraid."

"But if you won't listen to me and obey me, then when troubles come you will feel alone and afraid. You'll go to pieces, like the house that was built on the sand. You won't know where to turn. So trust in me and obey me."

The grumbling workers

What shall I get if I follow Jesus?

ONE day Peter said to Jesus, "We left our homes to follow you. What reward shall we get?"

We ought to get more than other people, thought Peter.

"I'll tell you a story," said Jesus. "One day a farmer came to market early in the morning and called to a group of men looking for work, 'Go and pick my grapes!' He told them how much he would pay them, and the men were pleased. It was a good, fair price for a day's work.

"The farmer came back at nine o'clock and chose some more workers. He came

again at lunch time, and at three o'clock, and yet again at five o'clock. Soon afterwards the sun began to set, and all the men came to the farm to be paid.

"The five o'clock men, who had waited all day for work, were paid first. To everybody's surprise they got a full day's pay.

"The early morning men were delighted. 'We shall get even more,' they whispered.

"But they didn't. They all got exactly the same.

"The early morning men were very cross. 'We ought to have more than the others,' they grumbled. 'We worked all day. It's not fair!'

"'But I gave you what I promised,' said the farmer. 'If I choose to be kind to these others who waited all day, it's nothing to be cross about. Can't I do what I like with my own money?'

"God always gives us far, far more than we deserve, because he is so kind and loving. Instead of being jealous of each other, let's serve him because we love him – not because we want a reward."

"The first servant was clever and strong, and the king gave him five hundred silver coins.

The lazy servant

Is cleverness important?

JESUS was always specially gentle and loving with people who were weak or disabled, or who were not very clever. One day he told this story:

"There was once a king who ruled over a great kingdom. He had to go away on a long journey, so he called his servants together.

"'I'm going away,' said the king. 'But I want you to stay here and work for me. I'm going to give you each some money to use for me. You could buy seed and sell the crops. Or you could buy some sheep and raise a flock. See what you can do. All I ask is that you do your best.'

32

"The second servant was not quite so clever or strong, so the king gave him two hundred silver coins.

"The third was weak, and he could not work very hard. The king smiled at him and gave him just one hundred silver coins. Then he went on his journey.

"The months went by. The first two servants worked as hard as they possibly could. Perhaps the first servant raised flocks of sheep and gathered great harvests. Perhaps the second servant produced one flock of sheep and one field of corn.

"Sometimes they came across the third servant sitting in the sun.

"'What are you doing with your hundred silver coins?' they would ask. 'The king will soon be back.'

"'Nothing,' muttered the servant. 'I'm not clever like you. If the king had given me five hundred coins ... then I might have done something.'

"So time passed, and one day the king came home.

"Everyone was glad to see him. Very soon the three servants were summoned to the palace. 'I want to know what you did with the money I gave you,' said the king.

"The first servant stepped forward and handed one thousand coins to the king. 'I farmed and harvested with all my strength,' he said, 'and now I can give you back twice as much as you gave me.'

"The king was very, very pleased. 'Well done, good, faithful servant,' he said. 'You have done so well that I am going to give you a much better job. Come and share my joy!'

"The second servant came forward. Perhaps he felt a little sad. 'I can only give you four hundred coins,' he said. 'But I did what I could and I doubled what you gave me.'

"The king was very, very pleased. 'Well done, good, faithful servant,' he said. 'You did so well that now I am going to give you a much better job. Come and share my joy!'

"Then he turned to the third servant. 'What did you earn?' he asked.

"'Nothing,' muttered the third servant. 'I'm not clever, so I buried your money. Here it is; you can have it back.'

"Then the king was angry. 'You lazy fellow!' he said. 'I only asked you to do your best, but you've wasted your time and my money. Give your hundred coins to the first servant, and go away. I don't want servants like you.'

Jesus meant that cleverness and strength are not really important to God. What matters is that you do your very best with what you have.

The foolish rich man

What really matters most?

JESUS had been telling his disciples that they might have to suffer for following him.

"But don't be afraid," he said. "Even if your enemies kill your bodies, they can't touch the real you. Your spirit, the real you, will go straight to heaven."

But one man in the crowd wasn't listening at all. Suddenly he stood up and interrupted Jesus. "Master!" he shouted. "My brother has stolen some of my money; tell him to give it back."

"I'm not here to decide things like that," said Jesus. "But I'll tell you a story. There was once a farmer who had such bumper crops that he simply didn't have any more room to store them.

"Perhaps someone said, 'How about giving some to the poor and the hungry?'

"'Oh dear no!' said the farmer. 'I want

everything for myself. I know what I'll do. I'll pull down my barns and build bigger ones. I'll store so much grain that I won't have to work for years and years. In fact, I can probably spend the rest of my life eating and drinking and enjoying myself.'

"He went to bed feeling very pleased with himself.

"Midnight! The room was dark and quiet. Suddenly the farmer woke and sat up in bed. Someone was speaking, and the farmer knew that it was the voice of God.

"'You foolish man!' said the voice. 'Tonight you are going to die, and you cannot take anything with you. You will lose everything.'

"Everyone is foolish," said Jesus, "who thinks only about getting rich on earth and forgets about being rich with God."

Getting things for ourselves – money, big houses and cars – makes us rich on earth.

Giving, loving, and sharing make us rich with God.

The hungry traveller

Why doesn't God always answer my prayer at once?

IT was midnight and a man lay quietly sleeping. Suddenly there was a loud knock at the door. The man woke up and ran to the window. There in the street stood his friend who lived a long way away.

"My dear friend!" cried the man, and ran to let him in. "Sit down and I'll get you some supper."

"Thank you," said the friend. "I am on a long journey, and I am indeed tired and hungry. I knew you would look after me."

The man went to the kitchen. Imagine how he felt when he found there was nothing to eat – not a single crust!

"Wait a minute," he called. He slipped out into the dark street and ran to his neighbor's house.

Knock, knock!

"Please open! My friend has arrived and the cupboard's empty. Please lend me three loaves."

"Sorry," shouted the neighbor. "We are all tucked up in bed, and I'm not getting out. Please go away!"

Knock, knock, knock!

"Please lend me three loaves."

"Go away."

Knock, knock, knock!

"Only three loaves; my friend is so hungry."

"And I'm sleepy. Go away!"

Knock, knock, knock!

"Look here.... I can't stand this much longer..."

Knock, knock, knock!

The neighbor leapt out of bed. All the children woke up. They heard their father rush to the kitchen and fling open the door.

"Here, take whatever you want," he shouted. "Only GO AWAY!"

Even a lazy, selfish neighbor will give a man what he wants if he goes on knocking long enough. So what about our Heavenly Father, who is loving and caring?

We do not know why God does not always answer our prayers at once. Sometimes he teaches us something by making us wait. We know too that he wants us to keep on telling him what we need.

This is how Jesus ended that story:

"Ask and it shall be given you.

"Seek and you shall find.

"Knock and the door will be opened to you."

The proud Pharisee

How should I pray?

IN the towns where Jesus travelled there were proud men called Pharisees. They thought that they did not need Jesus at all.

They went to all the services, and wore nice clothes, and preached sermons and looked so good. But Jesus, who saw right into their hearts, knew that they were really proud and unkind and selfish. One day he told a story about one of them.

"A Pharisee went up to the temple to pray. He wore his best clothes and hoped that everyone was watching. He went right up to the front. *They'll all see me here,* he thought. *They'll think I'm such a good person.*

"When he prayed, he talked about himself. 'Thank you, God, that I'm so good,' he said in a loud voice. 'I'm glad that I am better than other people, and not like that awful man over there. I never steal, I stick to my wife, I put money in the collection. There's nothing wrong with me.'

"Meanwhile the other man was also praying. He had been dishonest, and he was feeling very, very sorry. He longed to start again, and for God to forgive him. He wanted to live a different sort of life. He crouched, crying about all the wrong things he had done.

"'Please God, forgive me,' he sobbed. 'Be merciful to me, a sinner!'

Which prayer pleased God most?

The second one of course.

Prayer is talking honestly to God, and the Pharisee wasn't praying at all. He was just trying to impress God. But he forgot that God knew what he was really like.

The second man was like a sick person coming to a doctor. He knew he couldn't change himself or make himself good. So he cried out to God, the only one who could help him.

And that's the sort of prayer that God loves to answer.

The ten girls

Will I be ready when Jesus comes back?

WHEN Jesus lived in Palestine, weddings were different from our weddings. The bride and bridegroom had separate parties with their special friends. Then, late at night, the bridegroom would go and fetch his bride to his home. All the neighbors and other friends would follow the bridegroom into the bride's house and feast with them. Everyone was welcome.

One day Jesus told his disciples a story about a wedding. He wanted to tell them that he would come back to this world one day, to take God's children home to heaven. He wanted to warn us to be ready.

"Ten girls wanted to go to a wedding feast. They dressed in their party dresses and sat waiting. But the bridegroom was very late and, one by one, they fell asleep.

"Suddenly they woke up. There was the sound of music, and in the streets a lovely lantern procession. The bridegroom was

coming.

"'We'll light our lamps and join the procession,' said the happy girls. Five lamps shone brightly, and the girls hurried into the street. But five lamps wouldn't light at all.

"'Wait, wait!' cried the second five girls. 'We forgot to put oil in our lamps. Lend us some of yours.'

"'We can't,' called back the first five. 'There isn't enough to share. Run and buy some for yourselves, and catch up to us. Hurry!'

"But it took a long time to find an oil shop that was still open. By the time the five girls got back, panting and puffing, the procession had passed. The streets were dark and quiet again.

"It was too late. Even though they ran to the house and banged on the gate, the doorkeeper wouldn't open it.

"'Go home,' he said. 'I don't even know who you are.'

"So," said Jesus, "be ready! For you never know when I may come back."

The generous king

How can I be good enough for heaven?

"LISTEN," said Jesus, "and I will tell you how you can be ready."

"There was once a kind king whose son was going to get married.

"'I'm going to give the biggest, best party ever for my son,' said the king.

"So invitations were sent out and the feast was prepared. Then the king sent his servants out to summon the guests. First they went to the houses near the palace and knocked on the doors. But no one seemed to want to come.

"'Sorry, that's just the day I have to go and inspect my new field,' said the first.

"'What a pity!' said the second. 'I've just bought some oxen, and I can't wait to try them out.'

"'I would have come,' said a third, 'but I've just gotten married. I can't leave my wife!'

"So the servant went sadly back to the palace.

"'No one wants to come,' he whispered.

"The king was angry.

"'These people don't know what they are missing,' he said. 'But the party must go on! Go to the streets where the poor people live, and say, "Anyone who likes can come to the king's party."'

"Off went the servants. They stood in the narrow little streets where barefoot children played, and they shouted, 'Anyone who likes can come to the king's party.'

"The people simply could not believe it!

"'Not me!' said one woman. 'I've got nine children.'

"'Bring them all!' said the servant. 'The king loves children.'

"'But I'm blind,' said a poor beggar. 'How should I find the way?'

"'Get someone to lead you,' said the servant. 'The king specially mentioned the lame and the blind.'

"'But what about clothes?' cried the people. 'We have nothing grand to wear.'

"'Don't worry!' answered the servant. 'The king has a beautiful wedding garment for every guest. Not even the best dressed person can enter without it.'

"So, on the great day, the people from the streets came in crowds to the palace. Some led the blind or carried the lame, and all the children were there. They came just as they were, in their poor, ragged clothes.

"But before they reached the palace they were taken aside to wash and dress in fine wedding garments. They looked beautiful. No one felt shy any longer.

"But there was one foolish man. He looked at himself and thought, 'I'm cleaner and better dressed than these others. I don't need a wedding garment. I'll go just as I am!'

"The gatekeeper tried to stop him, but he pushed past. 'My clothes are quite good enough, thanks!' he said.

"Later the king came in to welcome the guests. What joy! What laughter! Until suddenly the king noticed the man dressed in his own clothes. His happy face grew sad and stern. 'However did you get in?' he asked.

"The man had nothing to say.

"'No one is allowed in without a wedding garment,' said the king. 'I'm afraid you'll have to leave.' And the man went sadly out into the dark."

None of us is good enough to go to heaven as we are. But God loves us, and longs for us to come; so he sent Jesus to die for our sins. When we come to him and ask him to forgive us and make us clean, he will gladly do so. Then, of course, we are welcome in God's home. It is just as if God had given each of us a new set of clothes.

The sneaky enemy

Why doesn't God destroy wickedness?

WHY is there so much sadness and cruelty in the world? Why doesn't God stop it all? People asked this question when Jesus was on earth, and they still ask it today. So Jesus told this story.

"A farmer went to his fields in spring to sow his wheat. It was the best seed and the ground was good. The sun shone and the rain fell, and the farmer waited eagerly for the first green shoots.

"But the farmer had an enemy who hated him. One dark night, when everybody was asleep, the enemy crept silently into the field. He scattered thistles among the wheat. Up and down he went, laughing to himself. Nobody knew.

"But later, when all the crops started to sprout, the workers gazed at the field in dismay.

"'Something's gone wrong here,' they said. 'We'd better call the master.'

"The farmer came running. He stared at the spoiled field; lovely green shoots almost crowded out by prickly thistles.

"'An enemy has done this,' he said sadly.

"'Shall we try and weed out the thistles?' asked the workers.

"The farmer shook his head. 'You couldn't do it without pulling up the wheat,' he said. 'Let them grow together till harvest time. Then we can easily sort them out. We'll save the wheat and burn the thistles.'"

Jesus explained that God is like that farmer. He creates all that is good and beautiful. But Satan, the enemy, works hard to spoil it, teaching people to be cruel and selfish. God hates to punish and he loves to forgive. But one day, when Jesus comes back, God will wait no longer. Then good will be rewarded and wickedness will be destroyed for ever.

God hates to punish and loves to forgive – and he gives people time to be sorry.

The surprised friends

What pleases God most?

JESUS once said to his disciples, "I want you to imagine that time has finished and people from every country are standing before God. Just as a shepherd with a mixed flock calls his sheep into one fold and his goats into another, so God calls some people to stand on his right and some on his left.

"First, he turns joyfully to the ones on the right.

"'How glad I am to see you again,' he says. 'Do you remember when I was feeling so hungry and thirsty, and you invited me for a meal? Or that cold night when you gave me a blanket? I remember lying ill and alone – I was even in prison once – and you came and cheered me up. How kind and caring you were!'

"The right-hand people were very surprised. They couldn't remember any of this. 'Lord,' they whispered, 'how gladly we would have helped you, but actually ... we've never seen you before. There must be some mistake.'

"'Oh no,' said the Lord, 'No mistake! Every time you helped someone – even a little child – you were helping me. I was there all the time.'

"Then sadly he turned to those on his left.

"'Go away,' he said. "You are not my friends. In fact, I don't think I have ever seen you before. You didn't care at all when I was hungry and thirsty and cold. When I was tired and ill or in prison you didn't bother!'

"The left-hand people simply couldn't understand it.

"'Lord, when did we see you hungry and cold and ill?' they cried. 'If we'd known it was you, of course we would have helped.'

"'I was there all the time,' said the Lord. 'Every time you wouldn't help ... every time you didn't care ... every time you were unkind and selfish ... you were hurting me.'"

53

The rich beggar

Who is really rich?

JESUS had been talking to some rich people who thought that having lots of money and nice things could make them happy. But happiness springs from what you are, not from what you have, so Jesus told them this story:

"There was once a very rich man. He had a beautiful house, wore expensive clothes, and ate delicious food at every meal.

"Each time he went out, he noticed at his front gate a beggar who was too weak and ill to work. His skin was covered with sores, and he was terribly hungry. He sat there hoping the rich man would notice him and throw him some leftovers. But the rich man never bothered.

"Lazarus, the beggar, loved and trusted God. When he died he went straight to God's home of love, where there is no more suffering. Lazarus was so happy, talking to all the others who had loved and trusted God, such as Abraham and David and Daniel.

"Then the rich man died and had a grand funeral. But because he had never loved God or other people, he had no place in that home of love. He was shut out. And, just as the beggar had hungered for food on earth, so now the rich man hungered to share in the joy of heaven, which he could see from far away.

"'Why,' said the rich man, 'there's that beggar who used to lie at my gate, sitting right next to Abraham. Father Abraham!' he called, 'ask Lazarus to bring me a little water from God's home of love.'

"'That cannot be,' said Abraham sadly. 'It's too late; you had everything on earth, but you never loved or shared. So now you have no place in God's home of love. Lazarus had nothing but he loved me, so now he has come home.'

"In the end, who was really the richest and happiest?"

You can find all these stories in your Bible.

The busy farmer	Matthew 13:1–9
The discontented son	Luke 15:11–32
The missing sheep	Luke 15:1–7
The selfish farmers	Luke 20:9–16
The unforgiving servant	Matthew 18:21–35
The good neighbor	Luke 10:25–37
The worried disciples	Matthew 6:25–34
The two builders	Luke 6:46–49
The grumbling workers	Matthew 20:1–16
The lazy servant	Luke 19:11–27
The foolish rich man	Luke 12:16–21
The hungry traveller	Luke 11:5–13
The proud Pharisee	Luke 18:9–14
The ten girls	Matthew 25:1–13
The generous king	Luke 14:15–24
The sneaky enemy	Matthew 13:24–30
The surprised friends	Matthew 25:31–46
The rich beggar	Luke 16:19–31

Patricia St. John began writing as a child, and her first book,
The Tanglewoods' Secret (1948), was written for girls at
the school where she worked. This book won first prize in a writing competition,
and, like her next book, *Treasures of the Snow* (1949),
has been reprinted more than 20 times, made into a feature film and televised.
Soon after the publication of her first book, Patricia St. John left Britain for
Morocco, where she spent the next 27 years as a missionary nurse with the
North Africa Mission (now known as Arab World Ministries).
In 1983 Miss St. John became president of the children's charity, Global Care.
She wrote in all some 25 books, with translations into 36 languages.
Her books include *Nothing Else Matters*, which won the Children's Book of the
Year Award at the Christian Booksellers' Convention in 1993.
Patricia St. John died on 16 August 1993.

Photo by Gordon Gray